せがわ せつこ キルトの世界-Ⅱ
PROGRESSIVE QUILT

せがわ せつこ キルトの世界-Ⅱ
PROGRESSIVE QUILT

by Setsuko Segawa

Published by Mitsumura Suiko Shoin

Japan

せがわせつこ著

光村推古書院刊

Published by Mitsumura Suiko Shoin Co., Ltd. Kyoto Japan
© 1987 Setsuko Segawa
First Edition May 1987
PRINTED IN JAPAN
ISBN4-8381-0090-6

目　次
CONTENTS

はじめに
PREFACE

せがわせつこ
Setsuko Segawa

冬木立の中をかけぬける風は冷たく、耳の痛さを
感じる程なのに、水辺の鳥達は大きく翼を拡げて飛
び立っていく———。
　私の手は、つねってみても感覚がない程になって
いると言うのに、あの鳥達は平然として翼を拡げ、
冬空へはばたいては又、氷った水辺に戻って来る。
一時間半も、ベンチに腰かけてスケッチしている私
など、完全に無視して、思うがままにはばたいては、
時折り、水しぶきを上げている。自然の中で生きて
いる動物達の力強さに、又私は脱帽してしまった。

　さまざまな事との出逢い———
　何かに出逢う———
　誰かに出逢う———
　出逢いによって、人それぞれ、物の感じ方、とら
え方の違いはあると思うが、私も又、それを大切に
している一人だと思う。何かを見てハッとする瞬間、
やはり私なりに他の人が感じない何かを感じ取って
いるし、それを私なりに表現して見たくなる。形と
して、色として自分の流れを残しておきたいと思う。
言葉で言いつくせない事も、形も、感じたままを何
かに表わせたらといつも思うのである。それはリア
ルな表現の方法ではないかもしれないが、確かに私
の感じた色と、形だと思う。

　私の中には、静と動がいつもとなり合わせで同居
しているような気がする。自分の中にある静が、時
折り、動を呼び起こしたり、又、動が静を呼び起こ
したりするのである。
　心の高まり、沈み、平常心と私の心はいつもこれ

らによって揺れ動いている。誰にでもある心の流れ
と言えばそれだけで終わってしまう事かもしれない
が、私は心の動きを形として作品に出して行きたい
と願っている。

　時々、自然の動物達のように自由でいられたらと
考えているが、自然の中で生きる動物みたいには、
たくましく生きることが出来ない現状である。
　一人の人間としてロマンを追い続けて行きたいし、
又、ロマンを持って生きたい。むずかしいと思うか
ら、そう思うのだろう———。

The wind blowing through the woods in winter is so chilly that it almost burns my ears. Still the birds at the water's edge take flight with their wings spread wide. The icy air numbs my hands, yet the birds swoop nonchalantly across the winter sky and down again to the frozen shore. Flapping and splashing away as they please, they pay no heed to me, who has been sitting on a bench making sketches of them for an hour and a half. I am struck with admiration at the life force of animals such as these surviving in nature.

Encountering something…
Encountering many different things…
Encountering someone…

People interpret their encounters in different ways. I am one of those who places much importance on the significance of encounters. The moment I see something, I always attach some special meaning to that experience (perhaps more than other people do) and I try to express this feeling in my own way. In colors and in forms, I hope to preserve my own stream of emotion — — to express things beyond words and to convey forms beyond appearances, just as I feel them. The images I create may differ from the "real" shapes, but nevertheless they are the forms and colors I feel.

I feel as if passiveness and activeness exist side by side within me. The passiveness sometimes rouses the activeness, and likewise the activeness awakens the passive. From exhileration to depression and back again to composure — — my mind is always unstable in this way. It may be the same ebb and flow of emotion that everyone has, but I hope to give form to those feelings in my work.

From time to time, I wonder what it's like to be as free as animals are in the wilderness, but the fact is that it is impossible to live as dauntlessly as they do in nature.
I want to go on pursuing my own, individual dream, continuously and constantly. I know it's difficult — — and therefore seek it all the more.

一枚のカレンダーをめくると
そこには春が待っているだろう
フィルターをかけたような
やさしい春の陽ざしが
待っているだろう―――

❶春　告
Arrival of spring
Arrivée du printemps
1650 × 2220mm

❷部分（春告）
detail (Arrival of spring)

❸早　春
Cherry-blossoms season
Saison de fleurs de cerisiers
1550 × 2170mm

❹時の流れ
Time flow
L'air du temps
2160 x 1620mm

❺部分
detail

16

❻椿と扇面
Camellia and fans
Camélia et éventail
2250×1590mm

18

❼藤と扇面
Wisteria and fans
Wistarie et éventail
2210 x 1590mm

❽華の宴
Banquet of flowers
Banquet de fleurs
2470 x 2170mm

❾部分
detail

❿竹の里
Bamboo grove
Forêt de bambou
1560 x 2770mm

❶陽 春
Spring brilliance
Printemps brillant
1100 x 2040mm

❿雅びの歌宴
Elegant gathering
Réunion élégante
1960 x 1370mm

❸静夜の円舞曲
Waltz in the silent night
Valse dans le soir silencieux
2250 x 1650mm

❹部分
detail

❶⑤祈　り
Prayer
Prière
2210 x 2610mm

❶❻はばたき I
Flapping wings-I
Battement d'ailes-I
1750 x 2500mm

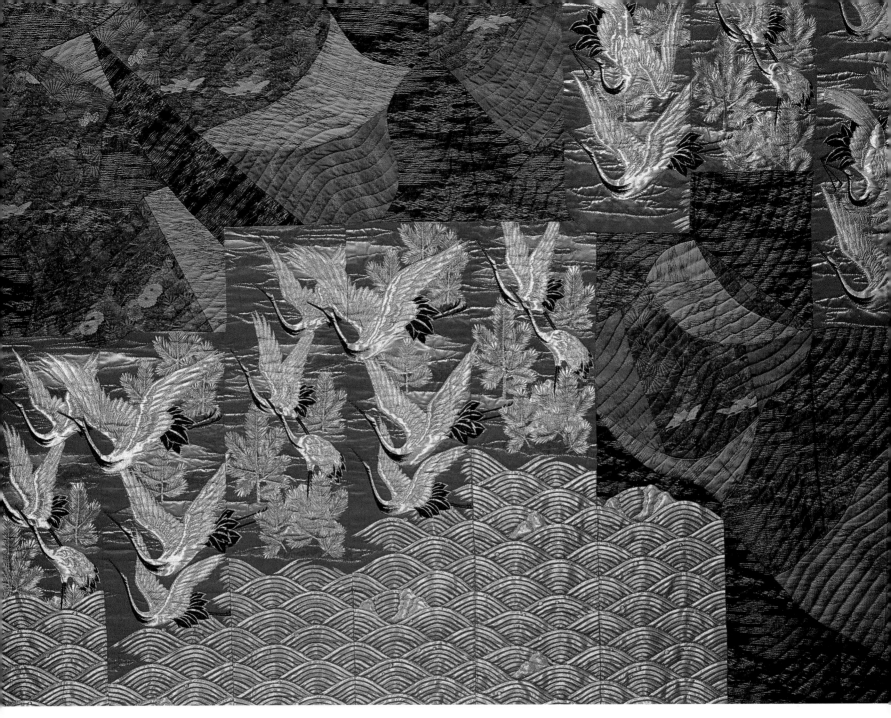

❶はばたきⅡ
Flapping wings-Ⅱ
Battement d'ailes-Ⅱ
2010 × 2590mm

❶晩秋の干潟
Late autumn tideland
La plaze en automne dernier
1610 × 1690mm

⓳何処へ

Where to?

Vers où ?

1550 x 2190mm

⓴部分

detail

大きく翼を拡げて
あの空の向うへ
旅に出て見たい——
何が待っているかを知るすべもないが——

㉑旅立ち
Departure
Départ
1560 x 2160mm

❷❷晩秋の宵
Late autumn evening
Soir du automne dernier
1630 × 2230mm

❷❸部分
detail

36

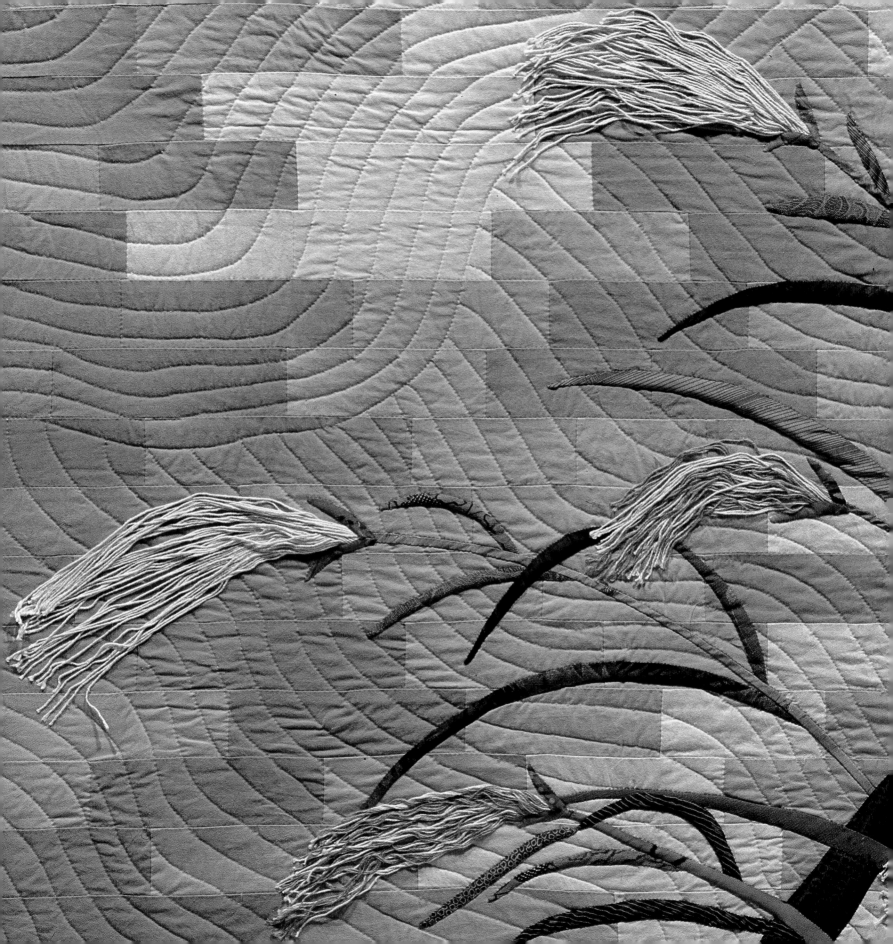

㉔秋・浮遊
Autumn, floating
L'automne, le cours
1620 x 2220mm

❷❺吹かれて
Autumn wind
Vent d'automne
1970 × 1680mm

❷❻部分
detail

40

㉗越 冬
Migration
1640 × 2210mm

㉘放 つ
Set free
Dénouement
1670 x 2080mm

❷⑨捻 転
Torsion
1520 x 1670mm

❸⓪部 分
detail

46

㉛ カラーハーモニー
Color harmony
Harmonie de couleurs
2020 x 1400mm

❸②流星の詩
Poem of a falling star
Poème d'étoile finante
2190 × 1180mm

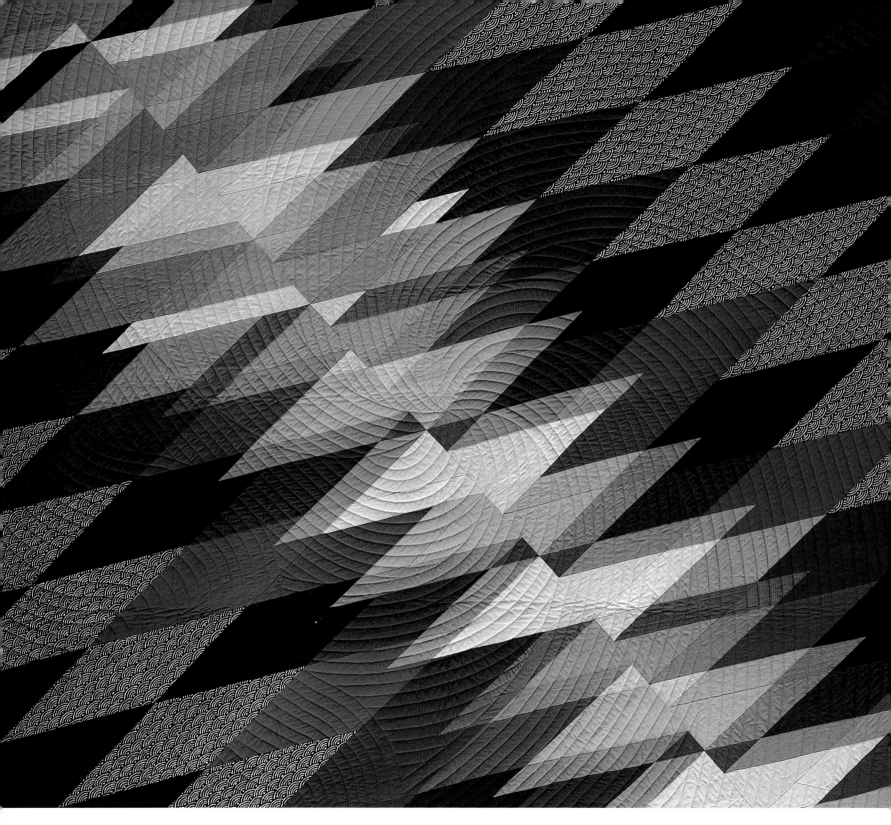

㉝エコー
Echo
Écho
1650 x 1910mm

㉞幻　想
Illusion
2220 x 1130mm

❸❺積木ゲーム
Game of playing blocks
Jeu de cubes
2010 x 1400mm

㊱マシンゲーム
Machine game
Jeu de machine
2010 × 1400mm

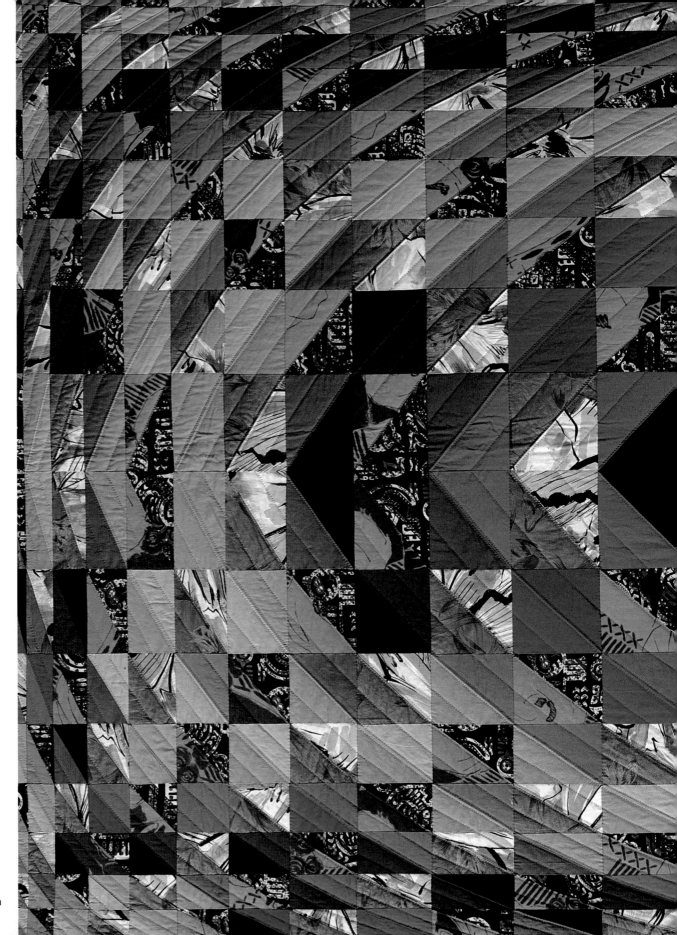

㊲瞳 奥
Inner eye
Fond d'oeil
1400 x 2040mm

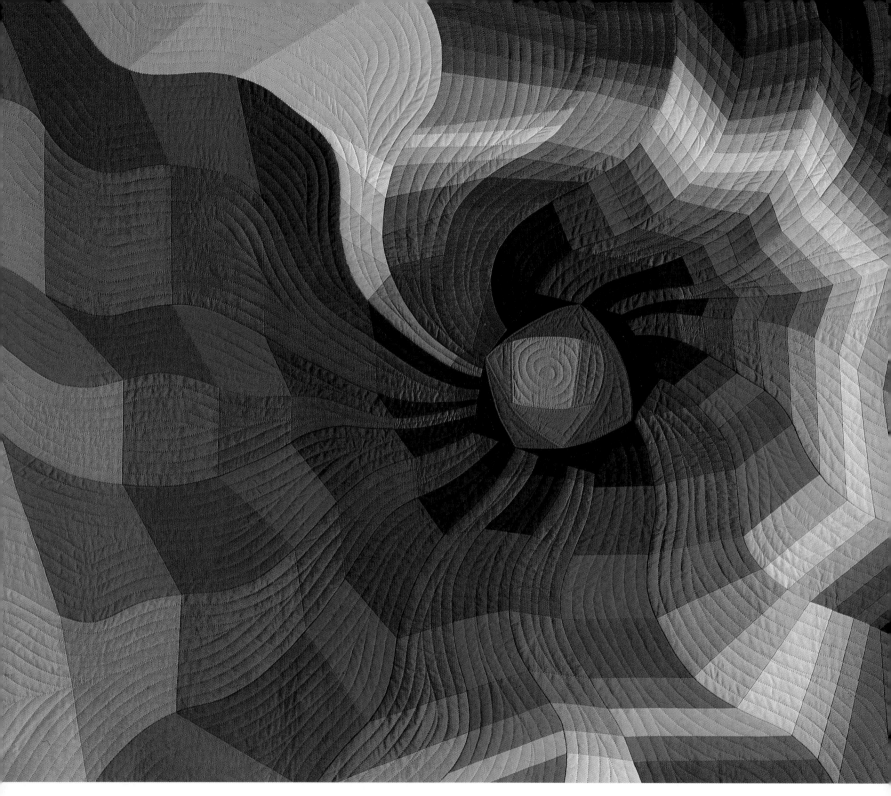

❸⓼周　波
Cycle
Fréquence
1440 x 2050mm

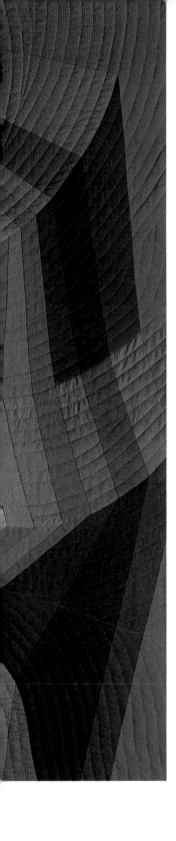

❸❾主　張
Insistence
Insistance
2020 x 1430mm

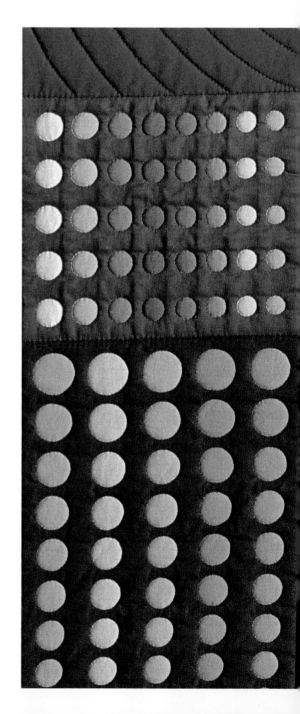

❹ X との対話
Conversation with X
Conversation avec X
2190 x 1130mm

無口でもおしゃべりでもないのに
何も話したくない——
何も聞こえない——
無の世界に時々、私がいる
聞こえないふりをしたのではなく
聞こえなかったのだ
心の扉が閉ざされた瞬間

❹部分
detail

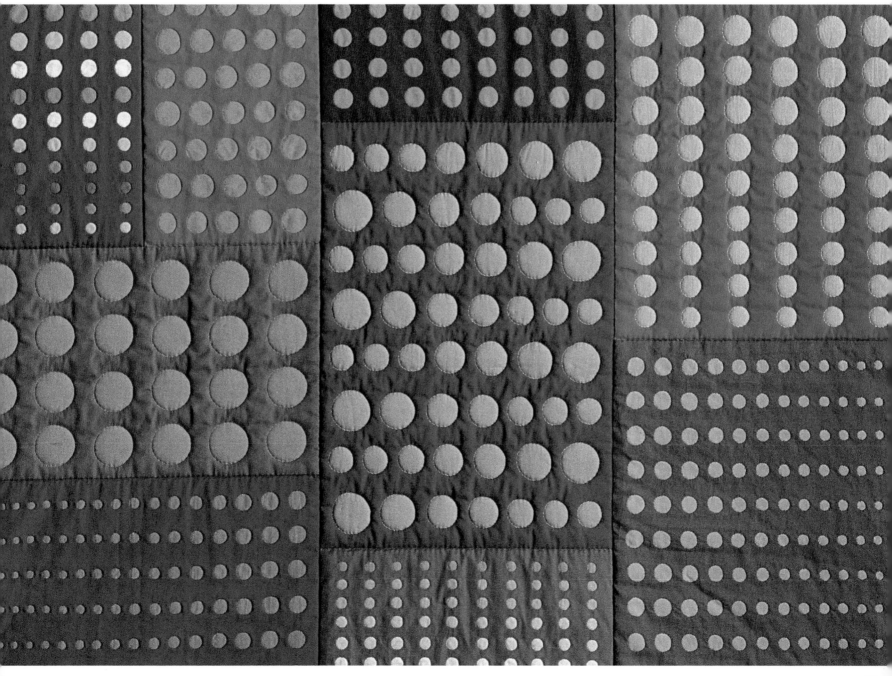

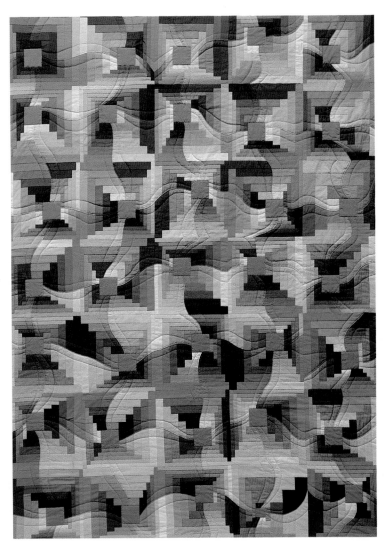

🞆ミステリアスな翼
Wings of mystery
Aile mystérieuse
2150 x 1570mm

🞆部分
detail

❹⑦ アールデコ・アンソロジィー
Art déco anthology
Anthologie de l'Art déco
2250 x 1880mm

❹⑥ ショー
The show
Spectacle
1650 x 1160mm

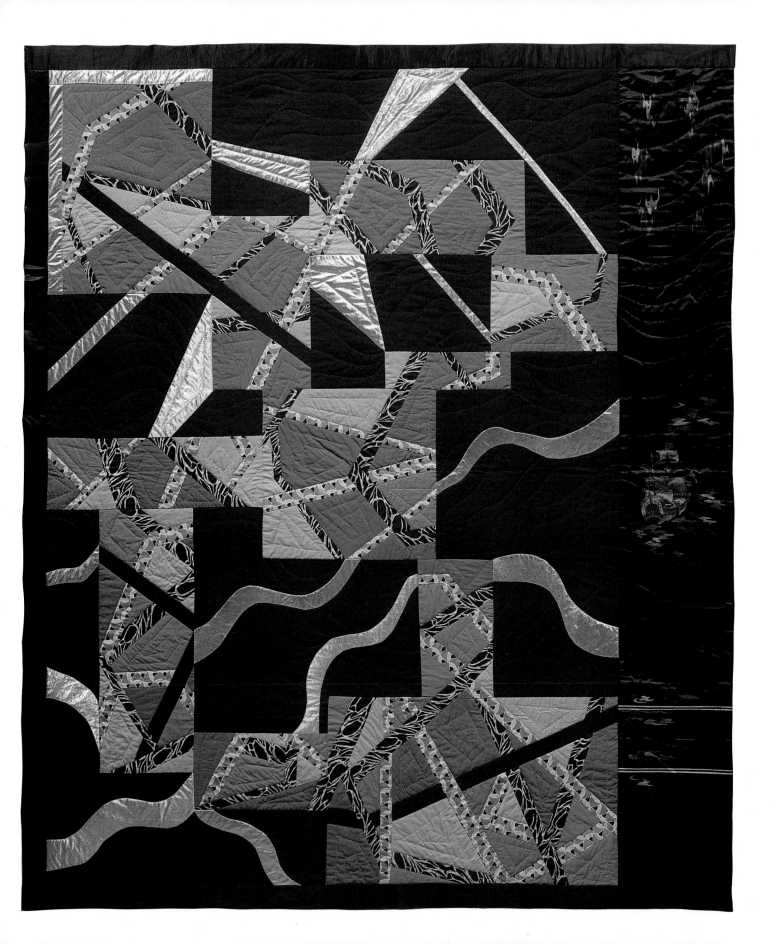

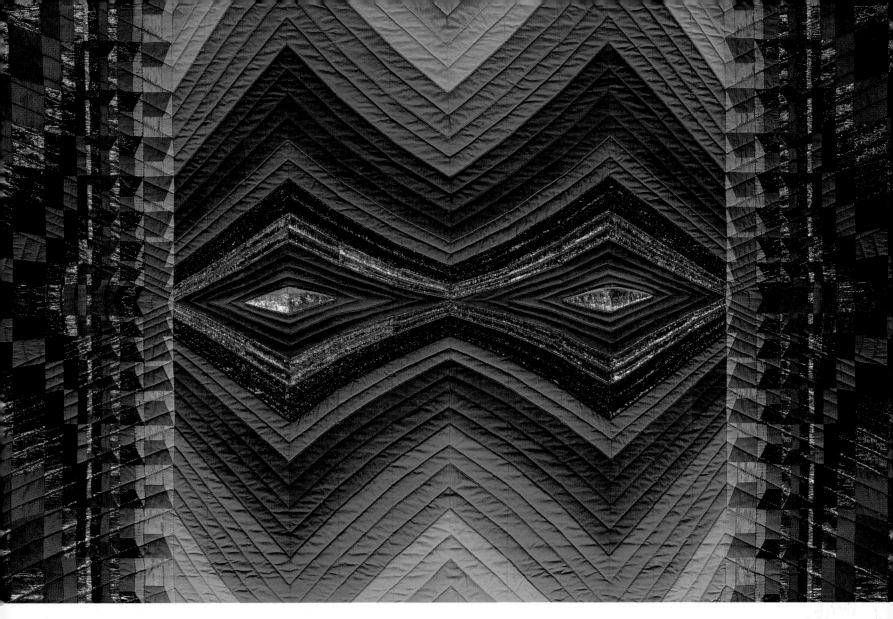

❹キャッツ I
Cats-I
1230 x 1890mm

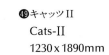

㊾キャッツⅡ
Cats-Ⅱ
1230 x 1890mm

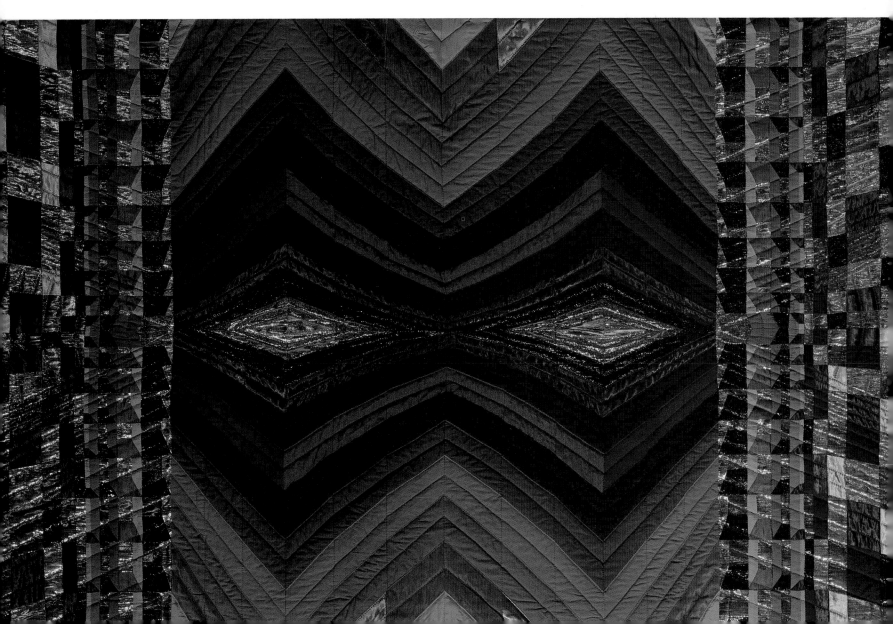

㊿キャッツⅢ
Cats-Ⅲ
1230 × 1890mm

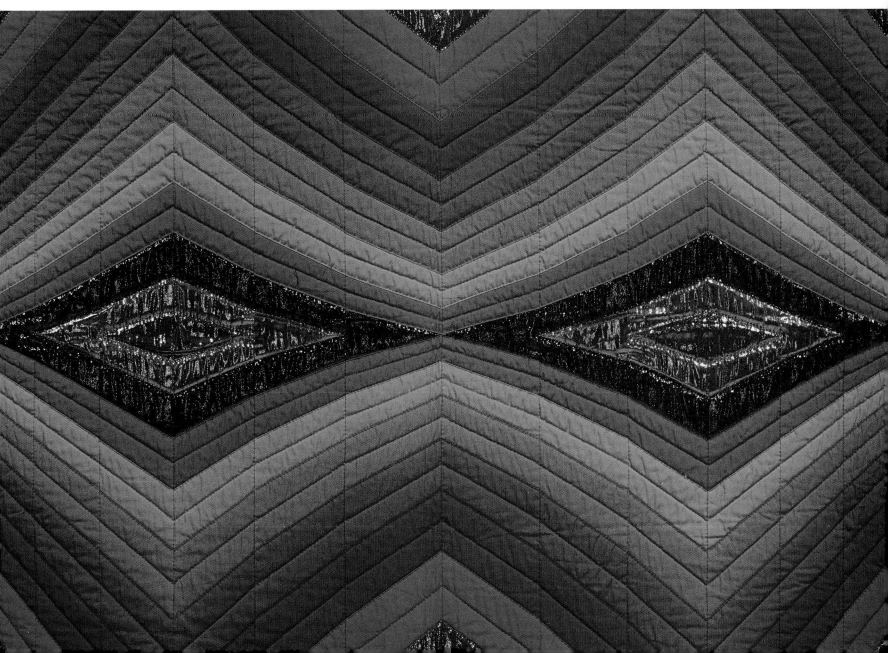

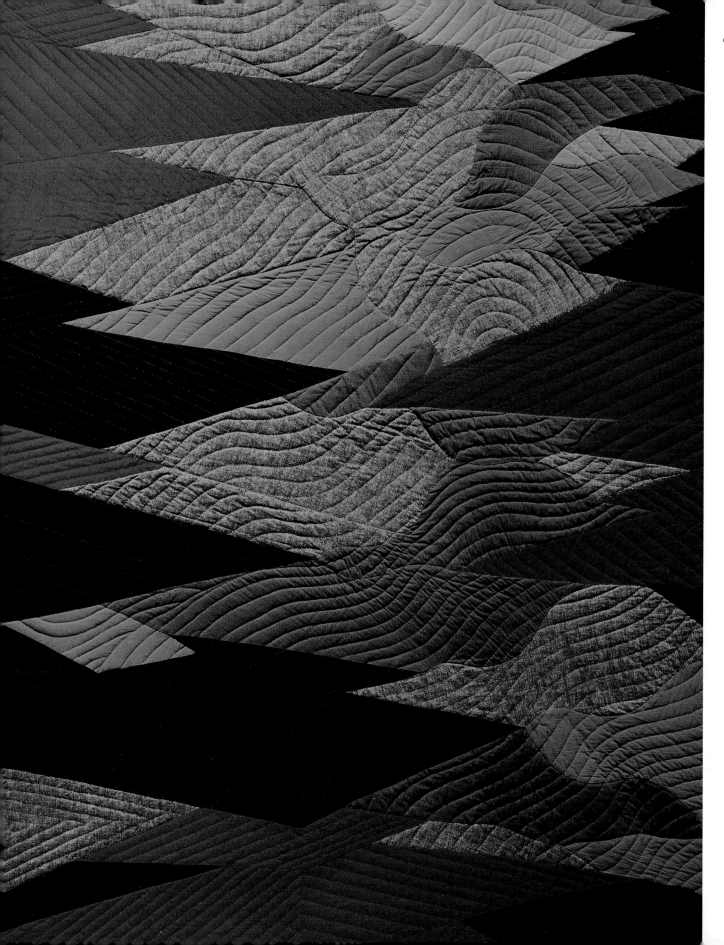

㉝秘めたる情熱
Secret passion
Passion secrète
2040 x 1590mm

㊸部分
detail

㊽モノクロームの風
Monochrome wind
Vent monochrome
1950 × 690mm

❺❺山 峡
Ravine
Ravin
2150 × 1110mm

❺❻大地の黄昏
Winter earth at dusk
Le crépuscule couvre la terre avec l'hiver
2200 × 1940mm

❺❼風は今
In the wind
Dans le vent
1390×1980mm

❺❽部分
detail

59叫　び
Horses' cry
Cri
1370 x 1970mm

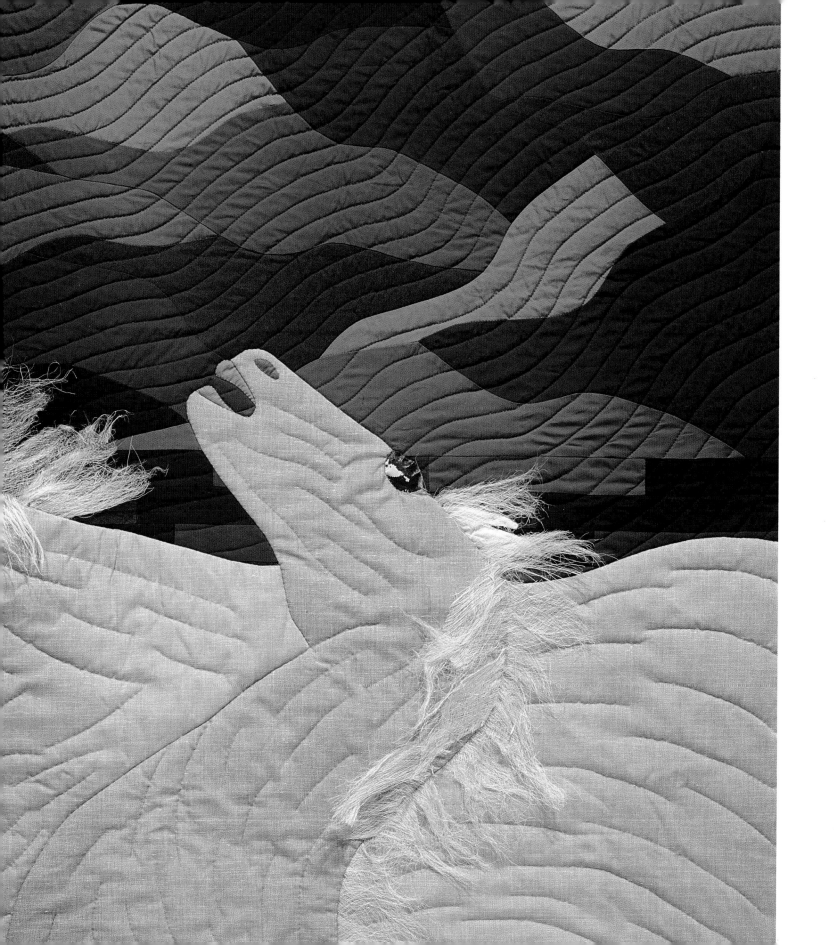

⑥炎華の宴
Fire feast
Banquet de flammes
1530 × 2060mm

⑥部分
detail

78

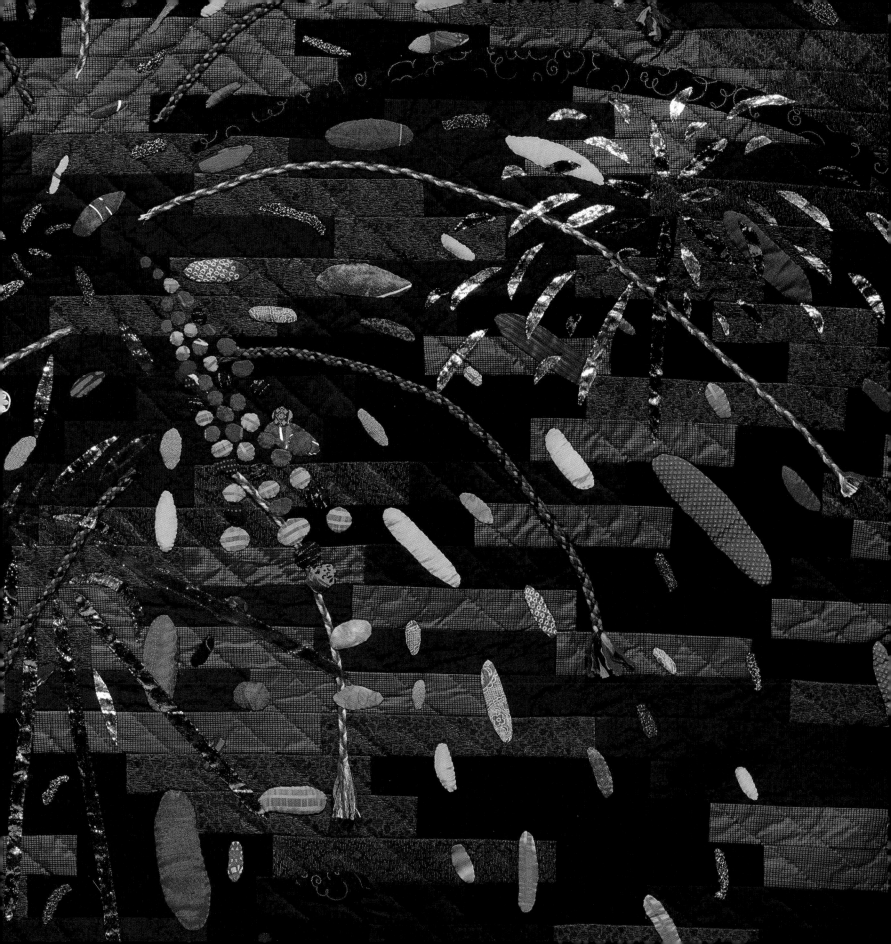

❻南からの便り
Southern wind
Vent du sud
1790 x 2070mm

南の海がすばらしいから──
見せてあげたいと
友より便りが届いた
見たいと思った──
行きたいと思ったから
出かけてしまった

64 憂 愁
Melancholy
Mélancolie
1600 x 1400mm

❻❺風の詩Ⅰ
Wind poem
Poème de vent-Ⅰ
1240 × 1670mm

❻❻部分
detail

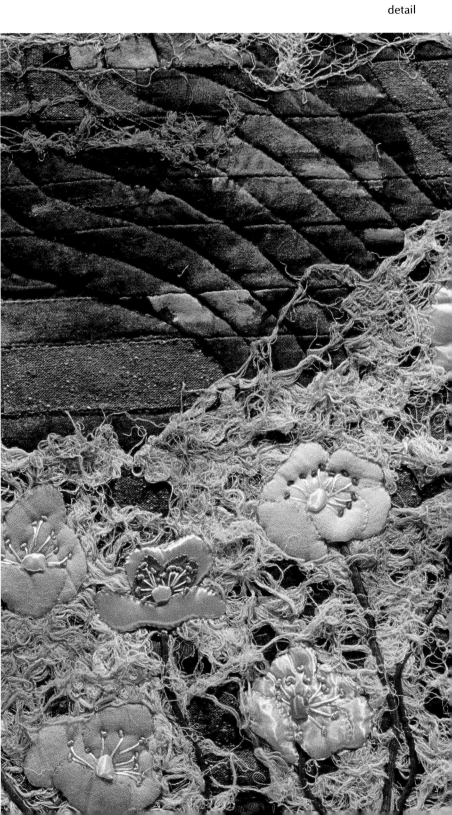

❻❼風の詩 II

Wind poem-II
Poème de vent-II
1220 x 890mm

作品解説

❶春　告
　桜と富士。通俗的な取り合わせではあるが、私には桜も富士も、見るたびに新鮮で心が動かされる。きっと、見ている私の方が、いつも少しずつ変化しているからに違いない。春の訪れを告げる桜にポイントを置き、全体にシルバーでまとめてみた。

❸早　春
　枝先に小さな春の訪れ。うっすらと頬をなぶってゆく風はまだ冷たい。あまりに小さな春ではあるが、来たるべき喜びの予感に私の心ははずみ、季節の扉を開く。まだ早い春のイメージをバックに、ほころび始めた桜をあしらってみた。

❹時のながれ
　時間が直線的に流れていくものとは、どうしても思えない。始めも終わりもなく、網の目のようにうねりながら錯綜する時間の流れ。その網目の向こうには、遙かな追憶の世界が垣間見える。———扇面と、テープをウェーブ状にして、時代の移り変わり、時の流れを表現してみた。

❻椿と扇面
　子供の頃、落ちた椿の花を拾って鼻にのせ、何メートル歩けたとか、花をつなげて首飾りを作ったり、髪飾りにしたりして遊んだ。幼い頃の思い出……。

❼藤と扇面
　優雅な花房をさげて咲き競う藤。万葉集にも藤に関する歌が数首詠まれており、大伴四綱の「藤波の花は盛りになりにけり平城の京を思ほすや君」や、山部赤人の「恋しけば形見にせむとわが屋戸に植え

し藤波いま咲きにけり」などがある。藤の花言葉は〝恋に酔う〟。まさに恋する色は藤色かもしれない。

❽華の宴
　花菖蒲は、私に落ち着きを与えてくれる。子供の頃、父がよく床の間に一輪生けていた。兄は、体の弱かった私に、いろいろな花のことを教えてくれた。この紫色の花を見るたびに、その頃を思い出す。
　3作とも、扇面と花をあわせて古典的なイメージを出した。前回の花シリーズの延長上にある作品。蝶の部分は帯柄をキルティングしたものである。

❿竹の里
　まだ誰も踏み入ったことのない森の奥深く。神秘的な泉のほとりに、群生する自然の竹林を見たように思った。バックの色は水辺。斜めに生えた竹や、からまった自然薯の蔓で野生の感じを表現した。竹には着物の生地を使っている。

⓫陽　春
　松も金色も慶事に通じる。松に慶びと古典的なイメージを与えるために、全体を扇面の形にした。新春の風も、ここでは金色に光り輝いている。

⓬雅びの歌宴
　うたた寝の夢枕に、何処からともなく聞こえて来る貴族たちの歌宴の音色。切れぎれに思い浮かぶ、懐しい絵物語の世界。———羽織りの裏を使った切り抜きの絵柄は、雅びやかな宮廷の絵。それに合わせて、百人一首の和歌を金糸の刺繍であしらってみた。バックの黒色が、明るい絵柄や金糸を映えさせている。

⓭静夜の円舞曲
　暗黒の闇を舞台に、一瞬満月の光に照らし出された雲の調べ。その合い間をぬうように、遠く近く舞い踊る鶴の群れ。いつか鶴の飛来地で見た光景を、夜に置き換えてみた。最初「鶴舞」というタイトル

を考えていたが、出来上がった作品には、もっと幻想的なタイトルの方が相応しいように思えてきた。

⓯祈　り
白無垢には女の幸せを願う敬虔な祈りが込められている。一方、般若の面には癒し難い女の業の深さが隠されている。女性の持つ二面性を表現してみたのだが、私自身に対する皮肉の表現といった方が当たっているかもしれない。中心に帯地を結んで、全体にアクセントをつけた。

⓰⓱はばたきⅠ、Ⅱ
波立つ水面、激しく震撼するまわりの空気。自然が垣間見せるダイナミックな美の一瞬の映像。一斉にはばたき、飛び立とうとする鶴の一群を、鮮やかな打掛の絵柄を使って表現した。

⓲晩秋の干潟
月あかりの下、風にそよぐ葦とたわむれる雁。万葉の昔から、さまざまな思いを込めて歌い継がれてきた晩秋の葦辺。その遙かな光景を、古代裂の額の中に収めてみた。

⓳何処へ
飛んで行く鳥達はどこへ行くのだろうか。たどり着く所が、彼らにとって幸福な楽天地でありますように。そんな願いをこめてデザインした。鶴の羽根には部分的に打掛と洋服地を使い、足はチェーンステッチでまとめている。

㉑旅立ち
私は、作品の中でも、ベースの色使いに細かい神経を使う。なぜなら、ベースの色でその情景が決まってしまうからだ。———ここでは、飛んでゆく渡り鳥の群れを生かす為に、背景に洋服と着物、そして蒲団の生地をアレンジして茜色にまとめた。

㉒晩秋の宵
月に薄雲、風になびくススキの穂。日本的な晩秋

の野地の宵をデザインした。ススキの穂は、綿ロープをほぐして用い、風になびく感じを出してみた。

㉔秋・浮遊
秋の水面を彩る気儘な風の指先。紅葉は、踊るように、歌うように水面のキャンバスに運ばれて行く。その流れるような動きを、そのまま捉えてみたいと思った。

㉕吹かれて
街路樹がセピアに彩づき、風に落葉が舞う頃、もし私が落葉なら、自然の風に吹かれて、寒秋のフィナーレを精一杯舞い踊るだろう。———バックの色、対角に流れる線の処理に神経を使った作品である。

㉗越　冬
厳しい冬の寒さに耐えて飛翔する渡り鳥達の、悲壮なまでの美しさと力強さを捉えてみたかった。バックは厳冬の空と海のイメージ。藍染の深い色が、鶴の白を一層鮮やかに浮かび上がらせている。

㉘放　つ
絞った布からヒントを得たデザイン。絞り込んだ布が、今まさに大空に解き放たれようとする瞬間である。力強くうねる曲線、濃紺の落ち着き、土佐紬のえんじ色が強いアクセントとなって全体を引き締めている。前作の「乱舞」の延長上の作品とも言えるだろう。

㉙捻　転
人生にはさまざまな紆余曲折があり、あらゆるものが複雑にからまりあっている。そんなイメージを、結ばれた布や解かれた布で表現してみた。バックのグレーはカメレオンクロスを、あとは着物の生地を使っている。

㉛カラーハーモニー
私を訪れる束の間の安らぎ。私はとても素直になる。優しく、懐かしい想いが私の心を満たしてくれ

る。そんな気持ちでデザインを描いた。グラデーションと、波うつ曲線で、色の調和や階調を表わしてみた。

❸❷流星の詩

　流れ星を数えてみたい。子供のような夢───でも、いつまでもそんな夢を心のどこかに持ちつづけていたい。眼を閉じて、まぶたの裏に残った星たちの残像を、永遠にキャンバスの中に閉じ込めてみたかった。オレンジ色の線や、星の形で流れ星の動きを表現した。

❸❸エコー

　私は、いつでも、私のリズムで生きている。ある時は耳で感じたり、またある時は目で、あるいは心で感じるリズムを表現した。中心の対角線は反響である。

❸❹幻　想

　私はカラーの夢をよく見る。そんな私がある日見た夢の世界。揺れ動く紫の帯は、私自身の心の表われなのだろう。出口を求めてさまよい歩く不安の幻影………。

❸❺積木ゲーム

❸❻マシンゲーム

　両方共、同じ構図のデザインだが、色によって全くイメージを変えてみた。

❸❼瞳　奥

　瞳を通じて、心の奥底のイメージをデザインした。さまざまな色に囲まれた中心には、ミステリアスな漆黒の世界──私の心のブラックホールがある。

❸❽周　波

　中心から発生して、波のように広がっていく周波。その中に、赤い一筋の流れがどうしても欲しかった。それが何故なのか、言葉で説明するのは難しいのだが………。

❸❾主　張

　単純なデザインをつなげたものだが、鮮やかな強い赤色で、私の中にゆれ動く情念の激しい主張を表現した。

❹❶Ⅹとの対話

　時々、ひとり言をつぶやいている自分に気がつく。無意味な言葉の羅列、泡沫のように浮かんでは消え……ふと気がつくと、無の世界の中心にたった一人でいる自分を見つけてしまう。円の列は、リバースアップリケで処理した。

❹❷起　源

　何かが起ころうとしている。誕生、あるいは変容への予兆に満ちた緊張。私には、起源のイメージはいつも不気味なものに思えてしまう。

❹❹ミステリアスな翼

　大空を飛びたい……少年が大空にあこがれるように、私にも翼があったなら……カラーのグラデーションによって、鳥の翼のイメージを表現した。パターンとしては、ログキャビンの変形である。

❹❻ショー

　水族館などで見るアシカのショー。芸をするアシカ達、出番を待つアシカ達、その素晴らしい芸と、一糸みだれぬチームワークをデザインした。

❹❼アールデコ・アンソロジィー

　アールデコのイメージを、布の素材と色の面白さによって表現した。フレームの船自体には特別な意味はない。

❹❽❹❾❺❶キャッツⅠ、Ⅱ、Ⅲ

　世界的に大ヒットしたミュージカル〝キャッツ〟は、そのメーキャップに特徴があった。そのキャッツ達の顔を、私なりにデザインしたものである。

❺❷秘めたる情熱

　無彩色をベースに、隠れた強い情熱を赤で表現し

た。赤の部分がもう少し増えると、私の心は止めどなく動き始める。

❸モノクロームの風

冬の風はモノクローム。私はモノトーンの世界にいるとき、安らぎを覚える。ヤーンを部分的に編んだり、縫いつけたりして、雪と樹氷を表現した。ところどころスパンコールを使って、雪の輝きを出している。

❺山　峡

明るい空をバックに、そびえ立つ山々。切り立った山脈は、私自身の心にある、峻厳で孤高なものへの憧れかもしれない。

❻大地の黄昏

冬の寒さの中、大地に雄然と立つ冬木の力強さを表現したかった。ベースをキルティングした上に、大樹をアップリケでまとめてみた。

❼風は今

風の舞う中、今走り出そうとする馬達。たてがみの処理は、シュロの皮をブリーチして色づけしたものを縫いこんだ。バックは染めた素材をつなぎ合わせ、部分的にポスターカラーを使用している。

❺叫　び

不安に包まれて、いななく馬達。動物の持つ鋭い感覚が、人間にはわからない異常をすばやく感じ取る。不安は不安を呼び、いま何かが起きようとしている。───たてがみには、最初ヤーンや布を考えたが、どうしてもイメージに合わなかった。シュロの皮を見つけて、初めて野生馬のリアルな荒々しさが出せたように思う。

❻炎華の宴

真夏の夜を彩る花火の美しさ、鮮やかさはまるで大空に咲く花のようであり、また一瞬で消えるはかなさは、何とも言えない情緒を感じさせる。その大輪の花をクローズアップでデザインしてみた。花火の線にはラメやコードを用い、部分的にヤーンや着物地を使っている。バックのベースは、男物の羽織りをほどいたものである。

❻南からの便り

いつになく心がはずむ。……南の空を、南の海を見たいと、友に語ったことがある。いつのことだったか記憶にないが、覚えていてくれた友がいた。私の心は南へかりたてられて、気がつくと機上の人となっていた。───椰子の葉は、シュロの皮を叩いてからブリーチし色づけをしたもので、葉のつけ根にはシュロの皮をそのまま使っている。バックは淡いトーンのブルーで、南の透みきった空と海のイメージを出した。

❻憂　愁

問いかけようか、やめようか、そんな迷いの表情である。言葉で表わせない寂しさ、憂いを色で、また物悲しい表情を目で表現したかった。肌には縮緬、髪にはカメレオンクロスを使っている。髪をグレーにしたのは、パープルとの調和を考えたからである。

❻風の詩Ⅰ
❻風の詩Ⅱ

南の空は、いつも私を魅了する。透んだ空の色を見ていると、遠く置き去りにされた記憶が呼び戻されるような気がする。その空と海の色を背景にして、花を表現したかった。花の群れやバックの波は、ガーゼを染めてから、一本一本ほぐしたものを縫いつけた、新しい手法である。

About the works

❶ Arrival of spring

Though it is a commonly used combination, my heart is still moved with a sense of freshness and renewal when I see Mt. Fuji with cherry blossoms. No doubt I change slightly each time I look at them. In this piece, while trying to give the quilt an overall silver effect, I used cherry blossoms to point out the coming of spring.

❸ Early spring

The tips of the branches have small spring visitors, but in the sky, a cold wind blows. I garnished the background's early spring sky with just-blooming cherry blossoms.

❹ Time flow

Somehow I can't conceive of time as flowing in a straight line. With no beginning and no end, like the mesh of a net, flowing time undulates and entangles. Over the net's mesh, I catch a glimpse of a world of distant recollections. The fans and streamers are used like waves in an attempt to represent the change and flow of time.

❻ Camellia and fans

❼ Wisteria and fans

❽ Banquet of flowers

Adorning fans with flowers brought out a classic Japanese image. This work is an extension of my earlier published flower series. The butterfly sections are designed from quilted pieces of *obi*.

❿ Bamboo grove

I imagined seeing a cluster of bamboo growing wild by a mysterious pond in the depths of a forest where no one has ever stepped before. The bamboo sections are made from kimono fabric.

⓫ Spring brilliance

The pine and gold color can be seen as signs of a happy event. To give the pine a classic sense as well as a sense of happiness, I used an overall fan shape pattern. The new spring's wind also shines in gold here.

⓬ Elegant gathering

Dozing, I dream; from somewhere I hear the sounds of a gathering of aristocrats. The pictures of an elegant Imperial garden are cuttings from the inside of a *haori*. These are combined with bits of Japanese *waka* poems embroidered in gold.

⓭ Waltz in the silent night

With the essence of darkness as a stage, from the full moon's light comes the melody of clouds. Flocks of dancing cranes far and near are sewn into the space. At first, I was going to title the piece "Crane Dance", but the finished quilt seemed to demand a more dreamlike title.

⓯ Prayer

A white Japanese wedding kimono contains a woman's devout wishes for happiness. On the other hand, hidden in the *hannya* mask is the hard to overcome woman's intuitive sense of foreboding. Though I tried to express something about the two sides of a woman, perhaps it's better to say this piece says something ironic about me. I used *obi* fabric as the main accent.

⑯ ⑰ Flapping wings Ⅰ, Ⅱ

Waves rise from the water's surface with a sense of rough vibrations in the surrounding air. A glimpse of the dynamic beauty of nature, a momentary image. All at once, wings flapping, the flock of cranes rises up to fly. I used the pattern from an *uchikake* kimono to express this.

⑱ Late autumn tideland

Beneath the light of the moon, reeds flow in the wind and wild geese frolic. By the reeds in late autumn, a variety of thoughts were inherited through songs from the age of the ancient *Manyo.* I tried to obtain the feeling of this long ago scene by using antique fabric.

⑲ Where to?

Where are these birds in flight going? I hope they come to a paradise of happiness when they find their way at last. I put this wish into this design. There are pieces of *uchikake* fabric as well as western fabrics in the cranes' wings; the legs are drawn by stitches.

㉑ Departure

I'm always worrying about backgrounds. Images of birds and flowers always float to my mind first. I felt that these and the sky colored base needed to be made the most of here. The background is from western clothes and kimono; I also used *futon* fabric in the arrangement.

㉒ Autumn, floating

The surface of the water is painted by the tip of the wind's finger. Acting as canvas, the surface of the water carries the singing, dancing leaves. I tried to capture this movement just as

it is.

㉓ Late autumn evening

Wispy clouds and the moon, pampas grass bending in the wind. I designed the Japanese image of fields in a late autumn evening. The tips of the pampas grass are made from untwisted cotton rope; this gives the wind blown effect.

㉕ Autumn wind

With the image of the blowing wind in back, I've drawn dancing, falling leaves. This work's main focus of concern was the treatment of the background color and the line flowing at an angle.

㉗ Migration

I wanted to capture the almost painfully sad beauty and strength of birds flying across the sky, enduring the harsh cold of winter. In the back is an image of the winter sky and sea. With the deep colors of *aizome,* the white cranes' brightness stands out all the more clearly.

㉘ Set free

This design takes a hint from the dappled cloth used. Variegated cloth is just right for expressing the moment of being set free in the sky. Powerfully undulating lines and the settled calm of navy blue. The strong red of the deep red *tosatsumugi* tightens up the piece.

㉙ Torsion

Life is filled with a variety of twists and turns, all ending up in a complicated entanglement. I tried to express this with pieces of cloth, some tied, some with threads loosened. The background gray is chameleon cloth, the rest is kimono fabric.

③① Color harmony

A moment of relaxation visits me. I become quiet and gentle. My heart is filled with sentimental remembrances. I used gradations and flowing lines to create a harmonic symmetry of colors.

③② Poem of a falling star

I want to try counting falling stars. It's like a child's dream, but I always want to carry that dream. I tried to capture the after image of stars on the back of my closed eyelids on a permanent canvas.

③③ Echo

Here I've represented a rhythm that is sometimes sensed with the ears, sometimes the eyes. The central diagonal line is an echo.

③④ Illusion

I often see dreams in color. This is what I saw one day in that dream world, a fantasy of the anxiety of roaming about in search of an exit. The shaking, moving purple *obi* is my heart.

③⑤ Game of playing blocks

③⑥ Machine game

Using the same composition and design, I used different colors to create an entirely different image.

③⑦ Cycles

Born from the center, cycles spread out like waves. Somehow I felt that I had to include the red line, but it's difficult to explain why.

③⑧ Insistence

Though it's a simple design, the sharp, acutely angled reds represent the harsh persistence and quickening emotions inside me.

③⑨ Inner eye

This design is an image of the depth of the soul as seen through the eye's pupil. There is a lustrous black world in the center of the many surrounding colors. Within my heart there is a black hole.

④⓪ Origin

Something is about to happen. An intuitive feeling of birth and change. For me, images of origins always carry a sense of eeriness.

④② Conversation with X

Sometimes I catch myself muttering to myself. Meaningless words line up; like bubbles, they float up and then disappear. Sunddenly I find myself alone in a world of nothingness. The lines of circles are done in reverse appliqué.

④④ Wings of mystery

I represented the image of birds' wings through color gradations. The pattern is done in a log cabin variation.

④⑥ The show

A sea lion show at an aquarium, the performing sea lions, sea lions waiting their turn, their wonderful tricks. Teamwork of perfect precision is the focus of this design.

④⑦ Art déco anthology

The image of art déco. I represented this image through the eyecatching elements of the fabrics' make and color. The boat on the frame doesn't have any particular meaning.

④⑧④⑨⑤⓪ Cats Ⅰ,Ⅱ,Ⅲ

The makeup in the worldwide big hit musical "Cats" was special and unique. This is my design of the cats' faces.

(52) Secret passion

On a flat gray base, strong hidden passions are expressed in red. If there were just a bit more red, my heart would start moving, never to stop again.

(53) Monochrome wind

Winter's wind is monochrome. The times I enter a monotone world, I remember relaxation. Yarn is knit and sewn into the piece in places. Snow and ice covered trees are represented, with sequins used in places to show the sparkle of snow.

(55) Ravine

Soaring mountains with a bright sky as background. Perhaps this piece shows my longing and admiration for things lofty and austere.

(56) Winter earth at dusk

I wanted to express the strength and power of a winter tree standing serenely in the earth in the cold of winter. The background color is the sunset.

(57) In the wind

In the eye of the dancing wind, horses about to run. The manes are done in hemp which was bleached, colored, and then sewed into the piece. The background is a piecing together of dyed materials. I also used poster colors in some areas.

(59) Horses' cry

Anxious horses neighing. Something that humans can't comprehend is about to occur. For the manes, I first thought of using yarn or cloth, but somehow they Just didn't seem right for the image. I think that using hemp helped me catch the roughness of wild horses for the first time.

(60) Fire feast

The beauty of mid summer's decorative fireworks, so vivid they look like flowers blooming in the sky. I feel an unspeakable emotion from the sense of transiency when they disappear in an instant. I tried designing a close up of a large flower. For the firework lines, I used lamé, cord, and in parts yarn and kimono fabric. The background is of cloth from a man's *haori.*

(62) Southern wind

A peaceful thought, a happy feeling. I like this kind of scene. The palm leaves are done in hemp, beaten, bleached, and colored. For the palm leaf stems, I used the hemp as is. The light blue background gives the image of the clear sky and sea of the south.

(64) Melancholy

Should I question? Perhaps I shouldn't. This piece is a representation of that uncertainty. I wanted to express through the eyes a lonliness inexpressible in words, and to express melancholy through color. The skin is done in crepe, and I used chameleon cloth for the hair. I used gray for the hair to harmonize with the purple.

(65) (67) Wind poem I, II

The sky I love, with the sea's color as background. I wanted to express something about flowers. I dyed gauze for the waving bunch of flowers in the back. I tried pulling the gauze apart thread by thread and sewing it onto the piece as a new technique.

0　　150　　300 m/m

〝時のながれ〟の制作順序

1、実物大の紙に図案を描く。
2、トレーシングペーパーにデザインを写す。
3、厚紙で型紙を作り、一つ一つに番号をふる。同様に
　　図案にも番号をふる。
4、色決めをする。
5、型紙に1cmの縫い代をつけて布を裁つ。
6、ベースをつなぎ合わせて、キルトをする。
7、キルトをしたベースに、図案を参照しながらキルト
　　綿を抱きこんで、アップリケをする。
8、アップリケのまわりに落しキルトをする。
9、扇面の部分にキルトする。
10、ふちをつけて仕上げる。

Directions for making "Time flow"

1. Draw the design on paper the actual size
   of quilt.
2. Trace the design with tracing paper.
3. Using the tracings, make pattern pieces
   out of cardboard. Number each pattern
   Piece and design section, being careful to
   match the numbers.
4. Select colors.
5. Add a 1cm sewing edge to the patterns;
   cut fabric.
6. Piece together cloth base; quilt.
7. Using original design as a reference, attach
   cotton-filled bppliqués.
8. Quilt along seams around appliqués.
9. Quilt the fan sections.
10. Finish the quilt with a hem.

P.46 ㉙捻 転 下 絵
Torsion design

0　　　　　150　　　　300 m/m

〝捻　転〟の制作順序

1、実物大の紙に図案を描く。

2、トレーシングペーパーにデザインを写す。

3、厚紙で型紙を作り、一つ一つに番号をふる。同様に
　　図案にも番号をふる。

4、色決めをする。

5、布をカットし、大きなブロックごとにつなぎ合わせ
　　る。

6、出来上がったトップにキルト線を書く。

7、バック、キルト綿、トップと三枚に重ねてしつけを
　　かける。

8、最初に落しキルトをし、次にキルト線にそって全体
　　にキルトする。

9、ふちをつけて仕上げる。

10、残っているキルト線を消す。

Directions for making "Torsion"

1. Draw the design on paper the actual size of quilt.

2. Trace the design with tracing paper.

3. Using the tracings, make pattern pieces
   out of cardboard. Number each pattern piece and design
   section, being careful to match the numbers.

4. Select colors.

5. Cut fabric. Piece together in large blocks.

6. Draw quilt lines on finished top piece.

7. Assemble top piece, cotton, and back; baste together.

8. First, quilt along seams, then quilt whole
   piece along drawn quilt lines.

9. Finish the quilt with a hem.

10. Erase quilt lines.

あとがき

　車中から見る冬景色に心を奪われそうになりなが
ら、忙しかった発刊までの日々を振り返る。体調を
こわして何回となくダウンし、生徒達に図案を描い
て渡すのが遅くなったり、レクチャーする事が出来
ない時もあった。この作品集はそのような状況の中
でも、信頼してついて来てくれた生徒達の制作協力
があったからこそ発刊出来たと思っています。前回
の制作協力、今回の制作協力の方々、大変な御苦労
だった事、改めてお礼申し上げます。

　或る時は私が鬼に見えたと後で笑って話してくれ
た事は本心だと思います。「でも、あの時創ってみて
本当に良かった」と生徒達から聞いた時、人と人と
の信頼関係の大切さを感じ、目頭が熱くなるのを感
じるのでした。一つの事をやりぬくという事の大変
さは、これまでにも数え切れない程経験し、何回と
なく挫折してしまいそうになった自分を知っている
から、理解出来るのです。そんな時こそ、自分と精
神力との戦いなのかもしれません。

　この一冊の本が出来るまで数多くの方々の御協力
がありました。光村推古書院の本田社長、日販国際
部の石川氏、大阪での活動の場をバックアップして
下さる㈱松山社長、専務、名古屋の中尾先生御夫妻、
編集で毎回困らせてしまった高安さん他、光村のス
タッフの方々、忙しい合間をぬって個展を見て下さ
った多くの方々、又、各地での個展を取材していた
だいたTV、新聞各社の方々と、読者の皆様に紙面を
お借りして厚くお礼申し上げます。

せがわ　せつこ

制作協力

SEGAWA P.Q.M.A.会員　五十音順

秋山洋子	浅野逸子	犬飼弘美	魚谷牧子
内田美智子	有働登喜	大下エツ子	大原素子
川西多栄子	梶河泰子	数本正子	加藤美根子
賀茂サチ子	清川八寿美	小松冴	小山智津子
是松多鶴子	近藤裕子	高田恵美子	高柳裕子
竹安美知子	椿原克都子	時広満江	中尾幸子
八田由紀子	平野直子	藤田ゆり子	藤原ウタコ
仏石紘子	増田真知子	松浦正子	三澤範子
水野智恵美	南口恵美子	三宅尚美	宮澤道子
六岡京子	山下真美	山本詩子	湯本まちこ

教室・連絡先

大阪市西区南堀江1-7-1　㈱松山内
06(531)6451　（木・金・土曜日）
名古屋市千種区今池3-12-14　りびんぐらんど内
052(733)6663　（月曜日）
広島市安佐南区沼田町伴700-240　是松多鶴子方
082(848)1642
東広島市西条町寺家18-230　魚谷牧子方
0824(28)5389
福岡市中央区城内6-11　清川八寿美方
092(751)1778
宮崎市希望ケ丘1-1-1　園田みち子方
0985(56)3349
京都市中京区麩屋町二条上ル　光村推古書院内
075(222)0361

せがわ せつこ プロフィール

1946年生まれ。
多摩美術大学卒業後、ヨーロッパでグラフィック、
テキスタイル、インテリアディスプレイ、フラワ
ーデザインなどを研究する。
現在SEGAWA. P. Q. M. A.(パッチワークキル
ト アソーシェイション)を主宰して、東京、大阪、
名古屋、広島、福岡などで指導。又、インテリア
コーディネーター、フラワーデザイナーとしても
活躍している。

せがわ せつこ キルトの世界-Ⅱ
PROGRESSIVE QUILT

昭和62年5月5日発行

著　者　せがわせつこ

発行者　本田欽三

発行所　株式会社 光村推古書院

604 京都市中京区麩屋町通二条上る
電話　075－222－0361
振替　京都 6-2336

印　刷　日本写真印刷株式会社

ISBN4-8381-0090-6